Cubby
Mud is

1

Cubby Bear runs in a big mud puddle.
Mud is so much fun!

Cubby Bear jumps in the mud.
Mud is so much fun!

3

Cubby Bear sits in the mud.
Mud is so much fun!

Cubby Bear rolls in the mud.
Mud is so much fun!

Cubby Bear sees Fuzzy Bear.
He gets up and runs to her.

Cubby Bear gives Fuzzy Bear a hug.
His big bear hug gets mud on her.

Mud is so much fun.
But it is not for hugs!